PROCEED WITH
CONFIDENCE

PROCEED WITH
CONFIDENCE

lessons learned from a serial entrepreneur

A. Ray Dalton

with Andrew K. Straka

**New
Vista
Partners**

Twinsburg, Ohio

I want to thank my Lord Jesus Christ for choosing me to be His instrument, my wife for her endless support and love, and my five children for putting up with a dad who is always changing something. Thanks also to my partners, my friends, and my associates for believing in me, and their willingness to follow. May we all make a difference.

For we are God's workmanship, created in Christ Jesus to do good works, which God prepared in advance for us to do.
Ephesians 2:10

Contents

PROCEED WITH
CONFIDENCE

Prologue

"Leadership is a matter of having people look at you and gain confidence, seeing how you react. If you're in control, they're in control." —*Tom Landry*

As a Christian husband, father, and respected pillar of the community, I figure the best way to improve my family life is to stop sleeping around. In the last eighteen months I woke up in a bed that's not my own, one hundred eighteen times. I'm referring to business trips, of course. You see, I'm the CEO of National MD, a division of GE—the world's largest company, by market value anyway—and that's what men in my position do. We travel. But of course we don't fly coach to hardware conventions in Des Moines, we travel to "planning sessions" and product launches in Boca Raton; our hotel names don't end with *Inn*. Ours is a life of fancy cars, private clubs, and company parties in the Mexican Riviera. The extravagance shapes even our grammar, and we find ourselves using nouns for verbs, as in, "We winter in Playa del Carmen."

Can I really give this up? I've worked so hard to get here, and finally, I have arrived. I rub shoulders with people you see on TV and magazine covers—society's appointed gods and goddesses whose mere presence turns heads, hushes crowds and elicits whispers of excitement. I employ a legion of underlings of whom I feel a deep need to keep employed. I've got an expense account bigger than the GDP of many developing nations, and I'm no stranger to the playgrounds of the rich and famous. I've flown to New York just to have dinner in the world's finest restaurants.

As I sit here tonight—my home office where

I've worked late into the night more nights than I care to think about—I remember a time when it wasn't like this. Not even close…

My mother left us when I was eighteen months old, and I am fortunate that my elderly grandparents cared enough to raise me. Mom did return, eight and a half years later when she found her way back to our place in Missouri on a snowy February day, loaded us into a rickety station wagon, and didn't stop driving until we arrived in California. I never saw my grandparents again.

By this time Mom had remarried twice, but even then I knew my new step-dad would never be nominated for Parent of the Year. We lived in the Watts area of L.A., a part of town rarely confused with Rodeo Drive, and I learned to deal with physical and emotional pain. If I had to choose, I would take the physical pain; at least that goes away. Destitution, crime, and drugs were just a way of life, and what few jobs were available were never enough to elevate anyone out of poverty. Fortunately, I never lacked for clothing—my stepfather drove a truck for the Salvation Army, so I always had the pick of their latest fashions.

The best part about living in poverty is there is no class envy; everybody is poor. Naturally, it wears on you, beats you down. Layer by layer, poverty peels away your dignity, hope, and self-worth—it strips you of your ability to dream. In Watts, there's not a lot of expectation, and for many, success is defined by simply staying out of jail. If you earn an income in something that's legal, it means you're probably pumping gas or pushing broom. The pall that hangs over this environment permeates everything, even the schools. There were no motivational speakers to assure us of our unlimited potential, no pep talks to lift our spirits or encourage us about our bright futures, and no advanced placement courses. Why should they offer AP, who goes to college? I earned decent grades, yet not one teacher or guidance counselor approached me about the possibility of continuing my education. For that matter, I didn't know anyone who attended college, much less someone who actually graduated, so why would it even cross my mind? Sure, I'll go to college, right after I buy that oceanfront estate in Malibu. I figured my future was limited to whatever work I could find fixing cars or framing houses, so I dropped out of school my junior year to marry a girl who wasn't even pregnant.

I credit the Air Force for turning my life around after a recruiter encouraged me to take an aptitude test. What did I have to lose but a little time? Time was one of the few things I had. I took the test, and it seemed to go well. When I returned a few weeks later to discuss the results, the recruiter praised me for my high marks.

"Ray, you had great scores, especially in science and math. People like you are hard to find. With a little training, the Air Force can transform your potential into highly-marketable skills—you could name your career path."

Nobody ever told me I was good at anything. To a teen who had experienced nothing but failure and negativity, the man's praise was like God Himself telling me that I was important and that my life had value. I didn't care if it was a sales pitch,

I would find a way to make it work; I wasn't about to pass up this opportunity. So while many young men my age fled in fear of Vietnam, I proudly signed on to serve my country. What else does a kid from Watts have to look forward to?

You can call it luck or mere chance, but like everything in my life, I now consider it God's providence when the Air Force asked me what I wanted to study. Our brief conversation—and the makings of my destiny—went something like this:

"Ray, what do you want to study?"

"What's the longest program you have?" I simply equated education with the time devoted to it—the more months I studied, the more skills I would acquire.

"Radiophysics. It's a 38-month program, Ray. Pretty intense."

"What's radiophysics?"

"X-rays and nuclear particles, that kind of stuff. I'll warn you, though, it's not easy."

"That's what I want."
So that's what I did.

The military chiseled away at the mold of what I was and shaped me into what I would become. For the first time in my life, I earned consistent praise, and it was the first time I was rewarded for my performance. Unlike most government organizations, the Air Force employs a simple management style: if you perform well, you advance. I performed well, and I advanced. And the best part of my education was the practical application. I learned how to use and troubleshoot equipment, which not only boosted my confidence, it made me a hero with my superiors. I never tired of hearing, "I'll bet Ray can fix it." Usually I could. It was especially gratifying if I fixed something that might take a bureaucratic process months to replace.

Then life sucker-punched me again. We had a son, but medical complications caused such confusion with my wife that she was convinced the baby was not ours. She left, we divorced, and I was left to raise the baby on my own. The Air Force notified me that my pending commission would be void if I remained a single parent: either put up my son for adoption or leave the Air Force.

I returned to California as a civilian in 1979, where my military training made it easy to land a job as an X-ray technician in a southern California hospital. That hospital is where I met my wife Jan, the primary reason I'm successful today. I moved quickly through the management ranks and, while still employed with the hospital, tried my hand at my own medical service company. As if two jobs and a wife weren't enough, I used my GI Bill to add night school to the mix and earned a degree in business administration from Chapman College.

I grew bored with the routine and office politics of the hospital, but when it came to working with my startup business, I loved calling my own shots. I knew my medical supply and services company had great potential, even though my boss figured I was just another dreamer destined to go broke. When I finally took the plunge and stepped away from the safety of a steady paycheck, the exhilaration was like nothing else! I had found my niche as an entrepreneur. In the years to come I would form a company, build it up, sell it, and then repeat the process. That became the blueprint for my success, and those experiences shaped me and led me to where I am today.

And so on this night, I face a dilemma. If I resign, the rumors and innuendos will make the gossip tabloids seem like church bulletins, and I won't be there to defend myself. There will be murmurs of improper conduct, or that I was forced out, and some will call me a quitter. But if I stay, my obsession with work is likely to alienate my family, friends, and maybe even the Lord I claim to serve. Friends have hinted that I've changed, and Jan flat out tells me the same. What they don't understand is that it's just temporary; I've had a lot going on. As soon as I get back from Europe, things will settle down and I'll promise Jan…

A hundred and eighteen days away from home! I slam my pen on the desk. That's not only unacceptable, it's insane. So what am I afraid of, that I won't find another job? I've *created* more companies than most people have had jobs. If I resign, I could start that medical service business I've dreamed about. Am I so in love with the power and urgency of this position that I've become blind to the things that matter for eternity?

I'm going to do it. I'm going to resign. All I really have to lose is my pride, and that would be a good thing. I laugh out loud—the enormity of what I am about to do is nuts; nobody works this hard to have it all, and then just gives it up. Yet I know, and I've sensed this for some time now, that it's the right thing to do. I take a deep breath, remarkably at peace, and turn out the light. I'll tell Jan in the morning. I think it will make her day.

And so that is what I recall from a life-changing night in late 1997. My decision that night would have been easy had I known the future, but I'm thankful that God rarely offers us the easy path. It makes the reward that much sweeter. Since that night when I committed every aspect of my life to Him, God has blessed me beyond measure—professionally, financially, and spiritually. He has given me not only a vision and a purpose, but fulfillment through a life of adventure. My goal is that this book will help you find your own dream and adventure, and encourage you to proceed with confidence.

Chapter 1
Defining moments

"Whether you think you can, or you think you can't, you get to be right."—Henry Ford

What better place to start my life over than the beautiful San Diego area? Fresh out of the Air Force with new skills and a much-needed boost of self-confidence, this single dad was ready to take on the world. The first thing I did was scour the medical ads in the newspapers, and before long I had my first real job in the civilian world: an x-ray technician at a local hospital. The situation worked well—not only did my regular paychecks make me feel like a millionaire, but the hospital was near a Montessori school where I could leave my son, Jeff. I had come a long way since my life in Watts, but I never forgot where I came from. The terror that I might return was a specter that would haunt me for years.

I'll never forget the day when a new nurse showed up in our radiology department. Her name was Jan, and she was fresh out of nursing school at Purdue University, having traveled all the way from Indiana to join the ranks of Southern California's legion of gorgeous women. Jan was beyond beautiful, she was a goddess, and I knew in that moment that I would marry her one day. I even told a friend as much. Who could have known that it would take a life-threatening injury to jump start our relationship. I recall the day I woke up in agony…

The good news is that I wake up early before my alarm jars me out of bed. The bad news is that I am in severe pain. My side feels as if I just swallowed a hunting knife. Somehow I manage to crawl out of bed, and I immediately realize this is more serious than a side stitch. I'm not about to call a cab or pay for an ambulance, so I do what I can to struggle into jeans and sweatshirt and hobble out to my motorcycle. I plop Jeff onto my bike, and then secure him to the frame, using my belt as a safety harness.

"Hang on, Jeff, here we go!" I ride off as fast as I dare. I'm riding sixty miles an hour when the pain flares again, and it's all I can do to keep from passing out. Jeff has me in a death grip so I have almost no way to relieve the stress.

When finally I reach the emergency room parking lot, I am terrified that something is about to burst. At any second I expect to see my large intestine spring out of my gut and wrap itself around a no-parking sign. I try to get off the bike, but the pain is so intense I can't put my leg down! I try again, but I still can't support my weight. This is nuts—is a doctor going to jump on with me and perform surgery as we ride? I take deep breaths but that just makes it worse. So I continue to ride in circles near the entrance, honking my horn.

"Don't worry," I yell back to Jeff, "someone will be out to help us any minute." I lay on the horn again, trying to ignore how ridiculous I must look. They aren't going to help me; I think they're going to shoot me for threatening their emergency room.

I remember someone saying, "Your appendix burst, and we're going to have to take it out." For all I know, it was the janitor who offered the advice. At some unknown time later, I regain consciousness and behold the face of the most beautiful angel that I've ever seen—a face I am sure I have seen before… but I fade back to…

Periodically I awaken, and each time I see the angel. I open my eyes again, feeling stronger and more alert. The angel is here again—and it's Jan! She tells me she worked overtime to make sure I was OK. My mental faculties are probably not their sharpest right now, but what she says sounds like a good thing.

When I return to work, Jan invites me to her apartment for dinner. "I'm fixing a turkey," she says, "and it's way too much for one person."

As if I need an explanation. But not wanting to appear too anxious, I ponder her offer for about two milliseconds, and then say, "You bet I'll be there!" Some days I have such incredible verbal comebacks. I would have said yes even if she were serving road kill. *All right, I've got a date!* I have been so busy the last few years trying to make a life for myself and my son that I have almost forgotten about women. What few opportunities I had were dashed the moment they discovered that I had a child.

On the day of the big meal, I strut like a peacock and show up at Jan's apartment with a dozen roses and a bottle of wine. This is how a ladies man does it; man, is she going to be impressed! Jan opens the door part way. She is still in her bathrobe.

"Ray! You're a little early…"

"You didn't tell me what time you were having dinner, and… well, I didn't want to be late."

"Ray, it's seven-thirty in the morning. I'm not even ready for breakfast—oh, those flowers are beautiful!"

"Just like the lady I'm visiting! Jan, I'm willing to help prepare dinner, or lunch, or breakfast. Really, I'll do whatever you need."

Maybe it's my puppy dog eyes, or maybe she just feels sorry for this poor bachelor. Whatever it is, it works, and she invites me in. We have great conversation and spend a delightful day together.

After that day, it didn't take long for me to find excuses to meet her, and soon Jan and I were dating. Her companionship not only brightened my days, she was a constant source of encouragement. Jan believed in me and saw potential that I never knew existed. I'll never forget the day we were discussing our careers, because it changed me forever.

"Ray, you can do more."

"What do you mean?"

"You're more than just an x-ray technician— you're bright, you're ambitious—look at how much you've accomplished, and you're already running rings around your supervisors. You know you could be doing their jobs."

She was right about that. "So what do you think I should do?"

"Anything... everything! Don't be afraid to dream big. I know you had excellent training in the military, but you ought to get a degree; that would open doors for you. After that, the world is yours for the taking."

So, before I began my conquest of the world, I figured I better get my degree. I took her advice and enrolled at nearby Chapman College. I studied business administration, taking classes three nights a week. I also began to look for opportunities.

"Never bring someone a problem without offering your idea of how to solve it."

Not long after I decided to take my career seriously, I was promoted to Chief X-ray Technician and began to create "Rayisms," quirky sayings—based on my experiences—that I loved to share.

That first promotion quickly led to a Rayism that I use to this day: *never bring someone a problem without offering your idea of how to solve it.* Since I was in charge of procuring supplies for the radiology units, doctors were always asking me if I could sell them the same supplies for their private practices. That was strictly forbidden, but it gave

"Good ideas usually follow the money."

me an idea for a business opportunity and another maxim I'll elaborate on later: *good ideas usually follow the money.*

Not wanting to jeopardize my career with the hospital, I asked my boss if there were any conflicts of interest with my proposed medical supplies business. I explained to him that I simply wanted to tap into a market the big supply companies had ignored.

"Ray, as long as you're doing it on your time, I don't care what you do."

So, I called the hospital's primary supplier and

asked if they would give me the same discount they gave the hospital. I told them my plan to sell to

---

"The person closest to the problem may have the best solution."

---

doctors in private practice, a market this supplier hadn't bothered with because private practices didn't order enough to make it worthwhile. The company agreed to my plan, and I was suddenly

---

"Growth businesses are those that solve problems."

---

a business owner. Hence, my aphorisms, *the person closest to the problem may have the best solution,* and its corollary, *growth businesses are those that solve problems.*

I began to notice inefficiencies throughout the hospital, but correcting them was another matter. It seemed that any suggestion I made was met with contempt: department heads called me meddlesome and accused me of being naïve. During those reprimands, I often thought to myself, what do we have to lose—why not at least try it? The thing that bothered me most about my job was the difficulty in tracking all the service contracts. With at least one hundred vendors—each, it seemed, had a dozen numbers to call—I felt like I was always on the phone for something. Sometimes it took weeks just to get someone onsite, and even longer to find the obscenely expensive replacement part. It was

---

"Where there's chaos, there's profit."

---

a full-time job just to track the service records; what we needed was a single supplier who could service everything. Now there was a business ripe for profit, and an opportunity for another saying: *where there's chaos, there's profit.*

The more I thought about that service business, the better I liked it. I approached my boss with the idea, and you would have thought I had proposed that we offer a lifetime of free health care. His reply, however, became the second-biggest influence in my life, when he shook his head and told me, "Ray, you'll never make it in health care."

I acted nonplussed, but inside I was furious. There was no explanation why my idea was so stupid—couldn't he at least admit the concept was a good one? Was I the only person in the world not content with the status quo? I knew how to fix medical equipment; maybe I should create my own service company. I began to dwell on the idea and devise ways of how I could make that happen.

Jan's vision about my abilities proved to be prophetic. After a brief stint as the head x-ray technician, I was promoted to Administrative Director of Radiology. It was my first salaried position, and I felt like I owned the world. I loved the control and worked hard to excel. Not long after, they promoted me again to Associate Hospital Administrator where I encountered more responsibility, and of course, more money. This kid from Watts was suddenly doing OK—better than OK—and I wondered if life could possibly get better.

Chapter 2
Forever changed

"Wisdom is knowing what to do next; virtue is doing it."—David Star Jordan

"OK, OK… I'll go," I tell Marcia, my secretary. *My* secretary—I get a kick out of saying that—and I am still amazed at how far I have come from my life in the projects.

"And make sure Jan goes with you," she adds.

"I wouldn't think of attending without her," I say, wondering what I had just gotten us into. The secretary had just invited me, for the umpteenth time, to visit her church, and finally I had caved. The depth of my church experience was a Mass performed in Latin, and the only reason I even went there was so I could stop at Dairy Queen for a foot-long chili dog. With all the adversity I had endured, a spiritual life was the last thing on my mind. It's not that I was opposed to religion, I just didn't see anything practical about it. If God did exist, why did He let me suffer the way I did? I decided to let the theologian discuss those issues. I had a life to live, and after a lot of hard work doing things my way, things were starting to shape up.

Jan and I were beginning to think about marriage, so it couldn't hurt to look into a church for our family. That was really the only benefit I saw; churches provided stability for families. Actually, I wasn't even sure they did that, or if it was all about appearances. I guess I would find out this Sunday. If nothing else, I would appease Marcia, and she wouldn't have to pester me any more about religion.

Marcia must have told her pastor that Jan and

I were attending because the sermon was written just for me. I was the person he described who was trying to work my way to heaven by my good deeds. He said the Bible indicated that was impossible because we are inherently sinful, and therefore, separated from God. Our only solution was a personal faith in Jesus Christ. At the end of the service, I made that decision to accept Christ by faith. Two weeks later, Jan did the same, and we were married shortly thereafter. Neither of us knew how profoundly that decision in 1982 would affect our lives, and that we would never be the same again. That decision defines who I am and what I do, and it is the reason for my story.

Some will laugh at my testimony and accuse me of "blind faith," but if mockery is the worst I have to endure for my Lord, then I'll consider mine an easy life. As to my faith, there is nothing blind about it: it's logical and based upon reason. Certainly faith is required; the Bible says that without faith it is impossible to please Him, but every belief system requires faith. Even an atheist places faith in the findings of others. My decision to follow Christ was no different than the business decisions I've had to make: I study the problem, research for a possible solution, and then act on what I believe is the most logical course of action. Doubters should consider this: no person in history has affected the world more profoundly than Jesus Christ, and I've never known a Christian who regretted the decision to follow Christ wholeheartedly.

While my spiritual life shaped how I would conduct my life, my circumstances played a major impact on how I would earn a living. Becoming an entrepreneur was like breathing to me—it had been a necessary form of survival most of my life. When you have to pay rent as a ten-year old, you become creative on how you can make money. My job history includes delivering newspapers, pumping gas, mixing paint, fixing cars and reselling them, and framing houses. Even today, I'm always looking for opportunities. Many would-be entrepreneurs look to glitzy prospects for sources of income, but it's often the mundane and unglamorous jobs that offer opportunity and wealth. Everyone wants to own a café in Aspen, while overlooking much-needed businesses such as repairing medical devices, cleaning x-ray processors, or selling repair parts.

I traveled a lot when I was selling medical equipment and supplies in Southern California, and I noticed a lot of hubcaps on the roadsides. Unfortunately, most were along highways where it was dangerous to stop. As a young man always scouring for opportunity, however, the danger of onrushing traffic never scared me. I routinely pulled off the side of the road, snagged the errant hubcap, and then tossed it in my trunk. On weekends, I cashed them in at a hubcap dealer, where they would fetch as much as a hundred dollars apiece. It was far from glamorous, but it was easy money.

My time at the hospital proved to be a great source of ideas for raising cash, including collecting used x-ray film. I bought used silver nitrate x-ray film from doctors and then stored it in a barrel.

When the barrel was full, I took the lot to a silver recovery firm. They paid good money for the film because they could extract the silver and resell it.

My life is a testimony of looking for needs and then meeting them. If I noticed a process that could be streamlined, then I looked for a way to improve it. The concept always works, because a more efficient process always decreases cost and often makes the product better. And after a life of working multiple jobs to make ends meet, I was never concerned about my work taking over my life, and I certainly couldn't imagine having too much money.

Working at the hospital was a natural fit for my side business because my customers—the hospital doctors—came to me. When I got home from my day job as an administrator, I placed the orders that I received during the day. Jan tracked the billing and typed the invoices. It was a fun time for us that allowed us to work together, talk about our day, and just wind down together. Not only was this a relatively safe way to make money for our growing family, I developed business acumen and honed my sales techniques.

While I had no formal training, I had been selling since I was a kid, so it's only natural that I found myself involved with medical sales. During

---

"The selling starts when the customer says no."

---

this time, I coined another colloquialism, *the selling starts when the customer says no.* Most of my sales were easy because the doctors knew me and often approached me about supplies. I did make sales calls, though. If a doctor told me he had all the supplies he needed, I suggested related products or offered a discount on larger quantities. Other times I tried being creative by throwing in something free for orders of high markup items or for multiple orders and referrals. I did everything I could to not lose the sale. It was like a game, and it made the job that much more fun. I didn't have a lick of sales training—I flew entirely by instinct, and my mother-in-law often told me that I could sell ice cubes to Eskimos. Life was my laboratory;

I simply paid attention to how people interacted and cataloged mental notes of my findings. Many

---

> *"Excellent customer service always results in profit."*
>
> *"People become repeat customers when you solve their problems."*
>
> *"No order is complete until you say, 'Thank You.'"*

---

of those discoveries found their way into my own proverbs, such as these three I still use:

> *Excellent customer service always results in a profit.*

> *People become repeat customers when you solve their problems.*

> *No order is complete until you say, "Thank you."*

While these may appear to be common sense, they aren't so common in today's business climate.

Good customer service always results in a profit, even though the profit does not always go directly into the coffers of the one rendering it. Smart business owners recognize that satisfied customers are likely to become repeat customers, and they provide companies with an invaluable word of mouth advertising network.

No order is complete until you say, "Thank you." Politeness never goes out of style, and nobody tires of hearing kind words. Ironically, nearly everyone who takes the high road when dealing with difficult customers feels far better about doing the right thing than they do by stooping to the level of the offender. I've heard too many customer service representatives with confrontational attitudes, and who wants to deal with that? I wonder how many billions of dollars are lost each year because employees fail to be polite and professional. Ultimately, I knew that if I simply continued to do what was right, I would have success. What I would soon find out, however, was how difficult that can be.

Chapter 3
My faith is tested

"Character is much easier kept than recovered."—*Thomas Paine*

It's a wonder that I wasn't telling people that Jesus would make their lives perfect. Six months after I had made my decision to follow Christ, I was twenty six years old, and I just received an offer better than I could have dreamed: the VP of Operations for a major health care provider. In my mind, I was in no way qualified to take this job, and I even told the company that. But they believed in me and offered me the world, including a generous salary and a company car—pretty heady stuff for a twenty-six-year old. I needed to tell people about this Christian lifestyle, because my blessings were beyond abundant! My confidence grew as I threw myself into the job, and I learned what it takes to succeed with a big company. Or so I thought...

One day our chief financial officer rushes into my office waving a paper as if he had just acquired the deed to Fort Knox.

"Ray, I need you to sign this. Now."

"What are we doing, selling the company? What's the hurry?"

"Medicare stuff. It's a rush, we've got to get this out, so if you could just sign—"

"All right, set it here," I said, motioning to my desk top. "I just want to give it a quick once-over."

"Come on, Ray, why are you making this so hard? All I need is a signature; let's get this out of the way!"

Now I am beginning to get frustrated. I know

I don't have a lot of experience in this type of corporate environment, but I resent being treated like an intern. *I'm a professional, for crying out loud, and if I say I'll get it to you, I'll get it to you.* I need to defuse this before I say something I'll regret.

"Tell you what," I say, taking the paper from him, "I'll look it over right now, and then I'll drop by your office. We'll have it out of the way before lunch." I offer my best "fair enough?" facial expression, giving him about as much satisfaction as a cracker does for a starving man. I'm not sure what to make of his lack of patience, but the firm hired me to review these financial statements, and that's what I plan to do.

"I'll see you soon," he says, and then storms out.

A part of me wants to wait awhile, just to rub it in, but then I would be lowering myself to the same standards that had just irritated me. *Why the sudden rush on government work—did Congress just announce they were planning to file for bankruptcy?* I pick up the lone sheet and study it.

A cursory review indicates the company

overcharged the government by millions. Millions! That's a lot, even by insurance company standards. Maybe I'm overlooking something obvious, but a closer examination reveals a pattern of overcharges. Clearly, this is more than just a misplaced decimal point. Before I start running around screaming and accusing people of heinous crimes, I better get my facts straight. I make my way to the CEO's office and explain that the Medicare numbers are too high.

He sighs, and then confesses, "Ray, those are the numbers we're going to use."

"But they're wrong."

"I understand that, but those are what we need to use."

Need to use? What's that supposed to mean? My silence prompts him to say, "I'll tell you what, Ray, why don't you just take lunch—think about it, and then sign these when you get back."

As if on cue, his phone rings, automatically dismissing me as he picks up. Take lunch, and then sign the papers? As if a little food and refreshment will help me feel better about cheating someone out of millions? I call Jan to discuss what just went on, and she convinces me to come home for lunch. I shove some papers into my briefcase, slam the cover, and charge out of the building. I have no intention of returning.

After a meal I hardly taste, I gather a collection of financial documents I have amassed, and begin to study them. I pore over numbers and notice a recurring pattern of overcharges. I double-check the figures, but there is no doubt that the company has padded expenses and falsified billings for years.

> *"A man is known by the integrity of his word."*

This is the company I had pledged my allegiance to? I remind myself of a principle I've tried to live by, *a man is known by the integrity of his word.*

I call the chairman of the board, brief him on my dilemma, and request an emergency board meeting for the following morning. Jan and I pray about this predicament and ask for wisdom on what I should do at the meeting. One shouldn't call the chairman without expecting things to happen. That night the phone rings. It's the CEO of my division.

"Ray," the CEO says, "you don't want to have that board meeting tomorrow."

I hold the receiver in silence, stunned. What is this, the Mob? Finally I manage, "I think we really need to discuss this. We've got some serious problems."

"You'll have some serious problems if you have that meeting tomorrow, Ray. I'm just letting you know right now, that meeting will be nothing but bad news for you."

"Then I have to take that chance."

"You think it over tonight, Ray. Call me in the morning if you have a change of heart, and it will be as if nothing happened."

Always the one with the upper hand, he hangs up.

As is nothing happened? We could go to jail for this! My mind is made up, though. I won't be calling anyone tomorrow morning with a change of heart—I would have that meeting.

Despite my convictions, I don't sleep well this night. I toss and turn as I realize what I'm up against.

The following day brings sunshine, but the mood inside is somber as the board members gather for this unplanned meeting. The fact that I'm interrupting the schedules of power brokers is reason enough to set me on edge; the gravity of my accusation does nothing to alleviate my tension. There's no turning back, now.

I begin my presentation and offer supporting evidence of my findings. Despite the incriminating documentation, the poker-faced board members offer only blank stares, adding to the tension. In less than half an hour, I'm finished. Probably in more ways than one.

An uncomfortable silence follows. Finally, the chairman says, "Ray, everything you said is true. But there's something you need to know. Sometimes big companies do things that are difficult to understand, and this is one of those times. You have to decide whether or not you're going to be a big company man."

I let the comment hang, and then ask, "So what does that mean for me?"

"What that means for you, Ray, is that if you want to work here, then you need to sign off on this document."

My worst fears are realized, but it's what I suspected all along. I shake my head, and then say, "Then I guess I'm not a big company man. I'm sure you can find someone to sign that paper." I thank them for their time and leave, knowing I will never see this supposedly hallowed room again.

My mind is reeling as I make the painful drive back to my office. Even though nobody outside that board room knows what went on, I feel as if everyone I pass in the hall is whispering about what a failure I am. Minutes ago, I was the epitome of the American Dream, and now I am just another guy who needs a job. And quite frankly, I'm angry at God. Jan and I prayed for wisdom—we asked for His guidance, and we felt confident that taking a stand was the right thing to do. I thought He would intervene somehow instead of letting the bad guys win. How could a just God do that? *Lord, I took a stand for you, and you just watched me fail! I thought you always provided for our needs.*

In my office, I clean out my personal belongings, wondering when an armed guard would escort me to my car. Wait a minute—I don't have a car. My company car is no longer mine. Now I don't even have a way to get home.

My phone rings, and it's all I can do to muster the strength to answer. It's my former boss. He's so cheerful I want to strangle him.

"This isn't a good time to talk," I tell him. I decide to be honest with him and give him the ten-second version of what happened: "I just lost my job, and this is the absolute worst day of my life."

"Good, good!" he says, and I'm stunned.

"Did you just hear what I said? I lost my job! I've got a mortgage payment that comes due every month, regardless of whether or not I have money, and I have a wife and two kids who would probably like to eat once in awhile, and…"

"Ray" he says, cutting me off, "I understand. What I mean is that it's good that you're available. I'm calling because a position just became available: the Sales Manager for San Diego. You would be perfect for it."

"If you're joking, your timing couldn't have been worse. This really is the worst day of my life and—"

"Of course I'm serious! Look, I'll put you on the company payroll right now, and then send a car for you to use. Keep the car until after the holidays, and if you decide that you don't want the job, just call me and we'll pick it up."

One year later, my unscrupulous former employer declared bankruptcy, and several key people were in jail. I can only imagine what might have happened to me, had I signed those papers. If I were writing this from a jail cell, my perspective on God's provision and faithfulness would likely be different. That ordeal—so bizarre that I couldn't have made it up if I wanted to—was a defining moment of my life. By stretching my limited faith, God showed His faithfulness by demonstrating that His ways are not our ways. At the time, I hoped I would I would never have to endure another test of faith, but that was just wishful thinking of a new Christian. God had bigger things in store for me.

Chapter 4

Nobody said this would be easy

"Character is doing the right thing when nobody's looking. There are too many people who think that the only thing that's right is to get by, and the only thing that's wrong is to get caught." —*J.C. Watts*

I've heard it said that success breeds success, and while that might be cliché, it was becoming true in my life. Naturally, I was convinced that my success was linked to more than just hard work and good luck. I discovered that the more I gave to God—my time, money, and effort—the more He gave to me. An old saying among Christians is that you can't out-give God, and that was certainly true for me. I continually found myself in positions of influence, and while I won't deny that I worked hard to make that happen, I know

---

"Manage your work with the intensity that you manage your life."

---

that the situations I found myself in were no mere coincidence. I learned that *if you manage work with the intensity that you manage your life, you will be successful,* so I made that one of my sayings.

In 1986, Jan attended a conference in Seattle for mothers of preschool children, or MOPS, as they affectionately refer to their organization. She was active in the ministry and jumped at the chance to visit an area of the country she had never seen. When she returned, my Hoosier gal from the flatlands was awestruck by the beauty of the Pacific Northwest.

"Oh Ray, it was so incredibly beautiful there! The smell of pine was everywhere. Conifers meet the ocean on craggy cliffs, and waves crash over sea stacks, there are white-capped mountains with snow, and—"

"So you liked it?"

She hits me. "It's more than just the scenery," she said. "Everyone is so laid back and friendly, and they're all into healthy lifestyles. Plus, I love all the cafes, and the bookstores and shops right on the waterside. We've got to move there!"

Move there? I've got a job; I can't just pack up and leave. "Well, it sounds great, but I would need to find work there," I said. I was sure her enthusiasm would fade, but as days passed, Jan's longing for the Northwest intensified, and she began to bring it up more often. Even then as a relatively new believer, I was convinced that God uses our spouse to help us make wise decisions. My experience had proved that, and I had learned that I would be a fool to ignore her counsel or her desires. The more I thought about moving up the coast, the better I liked the idea. But as friendly as the folks might be up there, they wouldn't appreciate supporting our family for free: I needed to find a way to earn a living.

I began to look for opportunities in Washington and Oregon. The only problem with my success was that the high-paying positions I was qualified for weren't available everywhere, or every day, for that matter. But at that stage in my career, I had an advantage: if a company doesn't want to hire me, maybe I could buy a company. That thinking led to an opportunity with a struggling x-ray supply firm in Eugene, Oregon, that I was convinced I could turn around.

I bought into the company, and, due to contractual obligations, we had almost no time to prepare for our move. To rectify the situation, a real estate agent would find us a temporary home so that we would have something ready when we made the transition to the Northwest. We told the agency we could be very flexible with the new place, but since we had four young children, we had two critical requirements: the home couldn't be on a hill and it couldn't have a pool. The hazards of a pool are obvious, but Jan didn't want to live on a hill because she feared runaway bicycles, skateboards, and other wheeled toys.

We arrived in Oregon to discover that the lovely abode the agent found for us was perched atop a steep hill. That didn't make a strong impression on Jan. The incredible view from the backyard pool did nothing to change her mind, either. In spite of our rough start, we managed to find a better-suited home on several acres adorned with fruit trees and a garden. We enjoyed the eclectic nature that college towns offer. Eugene is home to the University of Oregon, and other than its proximity to the ocean, the health-conscious Eugene was similar to Jan's experience in Seattle. We loved Eugene.

After I acquired my 49% share of the company, I learned a valuable lesson about ownership. My 51% partner was caught in several embarrassing and unethical situations serious enough that I needed to branch out on my own. When I told my lawyer about how I wanted to restructure the company, he quickly let me know what I was up against.

"Son, let me tell you something. You're strutting around acting like you're some kind of big cheese.

Owning 49% of a company is like buying one share of Pepsi and then demanding they change the color of the bottles."

We managed an equitable settlement where I could focus on my strengths—the service side of the medical business—and I created my next venture, Professional Radiographics. I was convinced that medical service was an untapped market, and I quickly found that to be true as we targeted small hospitals primarily on the West Coast. With our ability to deliver timely repair work, profits multiplied and the business expanded. This service aspect was becoming a familiar business pattern

"Rational thinking prevails."

that would eventually shape my life and form another axiom I've come to believe—*rational thinking prevails.*

It's ironic that to the degree that Jan yearned to move to this area, she began to long for her home in the Midwest. I understood completely, because our lives were changing. The carefree lifestyle that drew Jan to the West Coast became more complicated as she was now a mother of four. And grandkids need to see their grandparents, which was difficult when her family was two thousand miles away. I had no objection to the Midwest—I would move there in a second if it made Jan happy—but once again I had a successful business, and with it, many obligations. By now I shouldn't be surprised, but God was working to orchestrate a solution.

Several months later I get a call from a former boss, part of another familiar pattern that seems to follow me. He tells me he's with TRW in Chicago now, and that they want to expand into the medical service industry.

"Ray, this medical service division could be huge. We figure the fastest way to be successful is to start with something that works, so let us make you an offer on your company, and if you're willing to move to the Midwest, we'll put you in charge of the division."

"You're kidding, right?" *Chicago can't be more*

than a couple hours from Jan's parents!

"I'm serious. This will be a perfect solution for everyone, Ray; you can't possibly turn this down."

He was right. Within weeks, we had a deal, and the Dalton family was making plans for the Midwest. Once again, my life was stranger than fiction: I will make a profit from the sale of the company, we'll finally be near family, and I will have a great-paying job as General Manager of a Fortune 100 company. Plus, the division I'll head will enable me to work at what I love and do best. Considering what we have to gain, it would take something the magnitude of a world war for me to turn down this offer. And all of this from one phone call—and he called me! If I were a novelist, an editor would laugh if I tried to use this story as part of the plot line. I'm thankful, though, that we can't know our future. Had I known what was in store for me, I might not have had the courage to go.

Chapter 5
The price of integrity

*"If you have integrity, nothing else matters.
If you don't have integrity, nothing else
matters."—Alan Simpson*

Chicago is a couple thousand miles from
Eugene, but the Windy City is light years
away in culture. In 1987, we left the land of tie-
dye, yogurt, and bean sprouts for business suits
and meat and potatoes. I think there were more
hot dog vendors in Chicago than on the entire
West Coast. Chicago's concrete and nonstop traffic
stood in stark contrast to Eugene's conifers and

bicycle commuters.

We found a home in a northwest suburb about three hours from Jan's parents. I wasted no time in getting started with my new company, where I would head TRW's new medical services division. I was immediately impressed by the culture and discovered that the company was a vanguard of business ethics. I was going to like this new assignment.

As the division's Vice President and General Manager, I was excited to play a part in its genesis. It was a labor of love for me because I believed in its value. My belief played out as the services division became an immediate success. While I like to think I played a key role in that, I know the success was also due to the inherent value of its people. We simply met a need. Why go through a maze of hundreds of original equipment manufacturers when you can call one company to service all of your equipment? The fact that we did that faster, and for less money than the OEMs charged, enabled the business to sell itself. The concept of offering medical providers a single source for equipment had worked in the West, and it worked here. It would work anywhere, because every medical provider has similar needs. Oddly, not all customers recognize their true needs, but they are

> "The customer isn't always right, but he's still the customer."

still willing to pay for what they want. That quirk begat another proverb of mine: *the customer isn't always right, but he's still the customer.*

Every year the division grew, and about four years later TRW Corporate approached me about selling this business unit. They were selling numerous businesses unrelated to the aerospace or automotive industries. One thing I've learned is that I have to sever emotional ties to my creations. As much as I wanted TRW to keep my creation, I understand that life rarely goes as planned, so I went about trying to find a buyer for them. During this process, I wrote a business plan for a company I wanted to form that was a continuation strategy of the division I was about to sell. Considering how quickly TRW got offers, my future company could be in for a bright future.

It made perfect business sense for TRW to sell this division, especially since the offer was substantial. The buyer even offered to hire me to run the division, but I told them in what is now a frequently-repeated quote, "Anybody foolish enough to pay that much is not going to be happy with the way I run it." They probably wouldn't have taken it well if I had mentioned my adage, *rational thinking prevails.*

I make it a point to think through situations logically and consult the wisdom of respected colleagues. You would think that seeking wise counsel would be standard operating procedure for every business, yet I've seen so many intelligent people make rash decisions based entirely on emotion. Sadly, the emotion they base their decision on is too often fear or resentment.

I signed on with the new company with the stipulation that I'd be there for just three months to assist with the transition. They offered me a full-time position, and I might have taken it had I not encountered an awkward situation. I became aware of personal indiscretions on the part of my new boss that could have eventually affected me. He exerted considerable pressure on me to cover for him, but I refused. I desperately wanted the best for him, but he simply couldn't accept sound advice. It didn't take long before he had destroyed his marriage and any possibility of me working in that environment. It was time for me to leave.

The company, wanting to make things right and not call attention to the issue, offered me a million dollars in stock to stay. I declined. Some might say I was a fool—that I should take the money as a reward for my integrity and as a punishment to the

---

"The integrity of a man is fully tested when money is involved."

---

company. But I knew if I took the money I would feel as if I approved of the company's tolerance for unethical behavior. I could almost hear the rumblings… "Ray has a fit when the receptionist sneaks a pencil home from work, but put some cash in his pocket and he'll overlook the guy unloading the warehouse. Everyone has a price."

My integrity wasn't for sale. This was just one occasion that ingrained a credo that I often quote: *the integrity of a man is fully tested when money is involved.*

I assisted them in every way I could, but after ninety two days, I was on my own again and headed for a new adventure in Cleveland.

Chapter 6
Pieces of the puzzle

"Outstanding leaders go out of their way to boost the self-esteem of their personnel. If people believe in themselves, it's amazing what they can accomplish."—Sam Walton

Cleveland and Chicago are similar in their multi-ethnic makeup, their manufacturing heritage, and their love for sports. Chicago has far more traffic, Cleveland gets more snow, and both locales are worlds away from the West Coast. I had traded a new-age culture of yoga, sushi, and endurance sports for a life of polka, pierogies, and bowling.

In 1990, I arrived in Cleveland to rescue a struggling company, National Medical Diagnostics. National MD wasn't my first choice, but investors to whom I pitched my business plan wanted me to turn around their company—fast; yet another illustration of my motto, *where there's chaos, there's profit.* A man wandering through the desert isn't worried about the cost for a cup of cold water.

I spent the first year and a half settling lawsuits and paring the company from over two-hundred employees down to a dozen. "Maintenance" work isn't pleasant: I had been attracted to the business because it afforded me the opportunity to improve so many people's lives, including my own. At National MD, I felt as if I was tearing lives apart. But once we shored up the foundation, we acquired more investment capital and focused on my business plan of servicing medical equipment. This was essentially the plan I had pitched to the hospital back in California.

What we found was that most hospitals have so many service contracts that they simply turn over control to each department. That fractured oversight often means not only do hospitals pay too much for each service call, but they rarely coordinate the appointments. National MD's technicians could service all the equipment in a single visit. The concept worked, and within four years we had signed hundreds of hospitals, had no debt, and were exceptionally profitable. As a result, we became the nation's largest healthcare engineering company. The painful rebuilding had paid off, and it was a wonderful feeling of accomplishment.

As my career pattern seems to dictate, the original investors came calling and wanted a return on their investment. Naturally I was disappointed because we had worked so hard to build the company. But I understood—change is the nature of business. We sold the company to GE for an amazing return on investment, and once again, I went to work for the company that bought my idea. This was GE Medical System's first acquisition of a service company. I learned a lot at GE and consider it an honor to have served there. The company stretched me, enabling me to do more than I thought I was capable of, but I also discovered that a big corporation is just not my style. I am an entrepreneur at heart, and I knew it was time to return to my roots.

Once again I forayed into entrepreneurialism with a company called OneSource, a high-risk engineering services company located in a Cleveland suburb. Our goal was simple: to offer medical providers a single source for equipment repair of medical devices that could kill you. Staffed by biomedical engineers who could fix anything, the company specialized in the types of equipment that most companies don't want to deal with, such as laser, anesthesia, and endoscopy. OneSource also

"Add stock options to every employee compensation plan and you'll have a company run by owners rather than renters."

provided advanced analyses, like environmental testing and medical gas monitoring. As my modus operandi would dictate, OneSource was founded on my principles of following the money and meeting needs.

The company took off, and after three years and eleven acquisitions, I received an offer from GE: they wanted to buy OneSource. After removing emotion from the equation, I agreed to sell, yielding a significant return to the management team and its employee shareholders. I also discovered a principle that became a Rayism, *add stock options to every employee compensation plan, and you'll have a company run by owners rather than renters.*

"Treat everyone with kindness; you never know when you might have to work for them."

The sale benefited both parties and made me the first person to sell GE more than one company. The transaction also became the basis for how I want to interact with colleagues: *treat everyone with kindness; you never know when you might have to work for them.*

Of course that meant I needed a job, so I did what I have often done: I started another company. If nothing else, I figured I would like my boss.

Chapter 7
A new creation

"Hire people who are better than you are, then leave them to get on with it. Look for people who will aim for the remarkable, who will not settle for the routine."—David Ogilvy

I've learned to love Cleveland for its diversity, its natural beauty, and its spectacular change of seasons. As a former Southern Californian, however, I was still working on my appreciation of lake-effect snow in April. Cleveland was the perfect home for what I thought would be my retirement. At age forty four, I had six companies under my belt that I had developed and sold, so I figured the days of the frenzied lifestyle were behind me. So in 2000, when my son Nick and I signed up for our church missionary trip, who could have guessed it would inspire my next endeavor, a company I would one day call PartsSource…

After twenty four hours of bone-wearying travel, we arrive in Oradea, Romania, a city of nearly a quarter million people that dates back to 300 B.C. Our two-week mission is to build a house for an organization called Caminal Felix, a ministry that provides house parents and a loving home to orphaned children. I will be in charge of a roofing and framing crew, where I hope to make use of skills I learned as a teen. Almost as soon as we arrive, the man representing the orphanage informs me that Bob Padgett, the founder of Assist International, needs to see me immediately. I haven't been here five minutes and I already have a meeting? I came here to labor and get away from meetings. I can't imagine why anybody needs to see me, and I wonder at the urgency. But I remind myself that I am here on a mission trip, and the purpose of a missionary is to serve others. Dutifully, I agree to meet Mr. Padgett.

We meet inside our hotel lobby where Bob introduces himself as the president of Assist International, a humanitarian organization that sponsors health care projects around the world. They are also coordinators for support teams for the Caminal Felix orphanage we were assisting.

"Sorry about the rushed meeting, Ray, but I'm leaving for the States in the morning, and I have a major problem with some expensive medical equipment. I remembered from your application that you have a background in medical equipment, so you're my only hope."

"I'm not sure what I can do from here, but I'll try."

Bob explains that the hospital he is working with recently ordered cardiac monitoring equipment from a company called Marquette. Their dilemma is that not everything they ordered arrived, and GE just announced it is in the process of buying Marquette. Bob says he spoke with people at Marquette, but the company claims it can't do anything during this transition period, and that the hospital will have to work something out.

"This is a nightmare," Bob says, "there's no way GE's going to pay for something that Marquette was supposed to have done, and frankly, I don't have time to wait for their decision. Is there any way you can help me?"

"You might be surprised," I say, grinning, "I can try."

Bob raises an eyebrow.

"I know people at GE. I was the CEO of one of their medical divisions."

I wish I had a camera to capture the look on his face. Now I'm having fun, and this long day of travel seems like a small price to pay for an opportunity to serve in such a big way. "Look, I can't promise anything," I admit, "but I'll email GE tonight. I'll tell them the whole story, and then we'll pray that they can work out a solution." I am optimistic that GE will take the high road and honor Marquette's commitment.

During our conversation, Bob asks me about my goals for the mission trip and what I plan to do when I return home. He challenges me about what I will do with my life; whether I would be one to merely talk about my faith or actually live it through my actions. Bob looks me in the eye, and asks, "Are you an Ephesians 2:8-9 guy only, or are you also a 2:10 guy?"

He explains that nearly every Christian remembers Ephesians 2:8-9, the oft-quoted verses regarding salvation through faith in Christ, but nearly everyone conveniently forgets the following verse that transforms beliefs into actions: *For we are God's workmanship, created in Christ Jesus to do good works, which God prepared in advance for us to do.* I thought I was already doing good works; after all, I am on a mission trip. Bob reminds me that our trip, however noble, is only part-time. The question is will this adventure affect how I live my life?

I'm not much of a believer in coincidence, so there is no doubt in my mind that this situation was orchestrated by something bigger than all of us—the key contacts of two organizations don't just happen upon each other half a world away. Within twenty-four hours, I discovered that GE did indeed honor the Marquette contract. To this day, Assist International maintains a working relationship with GE; the giant company's dedication to service is reflected in their generous assistance to so many organizations around the world. Bob's question about what type of believer I am burned in my mind for months and his challenge eventually became the motivation for my life's work.

The need to live out my faith inspired me to create PartsSource, my most fulfilling company to date. PartsSource followed my familiar pattern of providing a necessary service at a discounted price. My track record suggests I am a visionary—I discover needs and have a sense for what is likely to be a need several years down the line. Not everyone agrees with me, however, and I remember discussing the PartsSource strategy with an OEM...

The representative shakes his head and tells me, "Ray, you should have quit while you were ahead. Nobody's going to buy used medical parts."

I smile, and say nothing. I'm confident, though,

that I'll prove him wrong. First of all, PartsSource is far more than just "used parts." We provide a needed service, a one-stop source for virtually every type of medical part, "the right part at the right time," as we like to say. Our goal is to lower the cost of health care and provide a worldwide ministry of health care to those less fortunate. Someone once likened our mission to providing a cup of cold water to a thirsting man.

I have never been discouraged by attitudes like that. As often as not, the barbs motivate me to prove people wrong. The world loves to tell people that big ideas are stupid. They are quick to assure you that your goal is unrealistic, or that if it is possible, then you're not qualified. This pessimism runs rampant today in science, politics, and virtually every aspect of our culture. If you choose to do big things or to work outside the norm, expect to hear contempt, ridicule, and scorn. There will be no lack of people telling you it can't be done.

I can't prove it, but I'm sure that every great achievement this world has known was met with opposition. Thomas Edison tested over six thousand plant fibers before he found a suitable filament that would burn for extended periods of time. Six thousand! What makes that all the more astounding is that there was no way that he could know for sure if it was even possible for a light bulb to burn for hours on end. I doubt there were many people who would have endured a thousand failures, much less six times that. One can only guess how the world might be different had Edison decided that his dream for reliable electric light just wasn't practical.

I started PartsSource with three men who were committed to each other and to the mission of the company: Charlie Koch, a faithful friend, advisor, and a man of integrity; Pat Fortunato, a committed Christian and loyal comrade, and my son Jeff. Over the last twelve years, I had worked with Charlie and Pat at National MD and OneSource, so we were starting our four-man team with a healthy blend of youth and experience. We saw the hand of God orchestrating circumstances that were clearly not by chance, right from the beginning.

Soon after my return from Romania, I got a call from a hospital in Pittsburgh that had heard about our ministry of recycling used medical devices for third world countries. They offered me their building full of equipment if we could take it within forty-eight hours. I was stunned that someone would call to give me something, but I had two major problems: I didn't have anywhere to put it or anything to move it. Even if I miraculously acquired a building, there was no way I could move everything in forty eight hours. I told him that I was indeed interested and said I would check on how I might make that happen. I wasn't about to say no. If I couldn't pull off a couple miracles, then I would make the sad telephone call to let them know I couldn't help them. But I was about to try every contact I knew to find a place to store those jewels...

My first phone call elicits an appointment with a friend I used to work with. I'm quickly ushered into my friend's office, where I explain my idea for the company I was starting. Then I tell him about the phone call I just received.

"So I need a warehouse, and I have to have it within forty-eight hours."

"Well, Ray, I just leased a warehouse because it was right behind us. I really don't need it right now." Manny reaches into his desk drawer, pulls out a set of keys, and tosses them to me. "Here you go. Now you've got yourself a warehouse. Just cover the rent and it's yours—starting today. By the way, the place is filled with old equipment that has either been donated or acquired on trades or credit—it's all junk to me. Use what you can."

I just look at him incredulously. "I don't know what to say; I'm stunned."

He's grinning now. "You don't have to say anything, just write that check! You're already late on your first payment."

Now that we have the building, we need to fill it, and in order to fill it, we need a forklift. I've never had to deal much with material handling, so this is a new frontier for me. That day I get a call from Pat's friend who informs me that a forklift company is going out of business, and that they are having an auction tomorrow. He isn't exactly sure how much the tow motors cost, but I get the impression that it is more than we can afford. We decide to go there with just $5000. If we don't find anything in that price range, well, we would be no worse off than we are now. If nothing else I would know what we're up against.

We arrive early and walk around the facility, eyeing the selection of twenty eight forklifts. A man asks me if he can help. He's the auctioneer. I describe to him the type of humanitarian work we plan to do, and he suggests an electric forklift. "You won't have to worry about propane tanks or venting your exhaust," he tells me. "If I were you, I would bid on Number 25 or 26. We'll sell them in numerical order, so you'll have to wait around a bit, but it will be worth the wait."

After they auction the first few forklifts, I grow increasingly nervous. Each sells for no less than $10,000, and one is $17,000. At this rate, my five grand might buy the wheels. Ignoring what the auctioneer told me an hour ago, I bid $5000 on the next tow motor, but I am outbid just seconds later. I try again with the next machine; same results. As the auctioneer's staccato rhythm catalyzes a bidding frenzy, I take a deep breath and compose myself. I determine to simply take the advice of a professional and wait my turn. If I'm outbid, so be it. I will have done everything I could do. I pray for wisdom, and I wait. My excitement builds as the auctioneer takes bids for number 24. I'm next! Finally, he asks for a bid for number 25, and the sing-song voice booms, "Five thousand, who'll give me five thousand..."

I jump on it. "Twenty-five hundred," I yell!

The auctioneer turns and points to me and booms, "Sold, for twenty five hundred!" He ignores the puzzled looks and mumbles, and then begins on forklift number 26. "Who will give me five thousand, five thousand... five thousand dollars?"

"Twenty-five hundred!" I shout.

"Sold for twenty-five hundred."

There are more murmurings, whispers, and shakes of the head. I don't care, I just bought two forklifts for an absurdly low amount we had budgeted for one. The auctioneer doesn't miss a beat and the bidding for the next machine continues. As I leave, he is busy accepting bids far higher than what I just paid, and I wish I could thank him. Something tells me he is part of a bigger plan than just selling equipment. The following day we ship the equipment from Pittsburgh into our new warehouse, and we are officially in business.

God's provision never stopped, and as we prospered, it was clear we needed more space. During this time of growth, I was still doing some consulting work on the side. On this day, I was to meet with a banker to help a company complete their requirements for bankruptcy. Bankruptcy is never pleasant for any of the parties involved, including me, and I wasn't looking forward to this meeting. After all, what good could possibly come from a meeting where you're deciding who doesn't get paid?

The bank official manages to make the discussion as amicable as I could hope for. We are knee-deep in settling assets, when he asks, "So, Ray, what is it exactly that you do?"

"I'm a part-time consultant, but my primary business is now in the medical parts industry. I've just started a company called PartsSource." I give him a brief explanation of how the company works and tell him how quickly we have grown.

"So you're looking to expand?"

I nod and say, "We're going to need something soon."

He pauses and dwells on that for a moment. Finally, he says, "We have a building that's available. It's fully equipped with phones, fixtures, and everything you need to run a growing business. If you're willing to take it right now and rent it for a year, you can have everything in it. That would solve a lot of problems."

Would that ever! I try not to show my excitement, but I feel like a six-year old who just won a toy store shopping spree. "I think you're right," I finally admit in what is surely the biggest understatement of my life.

"You'll like it, Ray, the building is in move-in

condition. It has a state-of-the-art phone system, a LAN, and broadband capability—you're good to go."

"Deal!" And so PartsSource acquires its second home as well as a banking relationship that grows with the company.

Chapter 8
A company with a purpose

"We make a living by what we get; we make a life by what we give."—Winston Churchill

One of the tenets of our startup company is a commitment to philanthropy. We decide that part of our ministry—and we consider everything we do as ministry—is to provide for facilities in cultures that cannot afford state of the art equipment or even the replacement parts to repair what they already have. One way we commit is to make our donations a top priority.

So if two facilities need a part at the same time, we give first choice to the underprivileged facility. I figure that will be a rare occurrence, but it's good to know we have a protocol in case it does happen. The Lord decides to test that commitment almost immediately.

A missionary organization we had developed a relationship with introduces us to Romanian hospital in need. PartsSource had promised to provide the hospital with an electronic circuit board that we typically sell for about $17,000. But the minute we acquire the part, a Pittsburgh hospital asks for that very board. It's a rare startup business that feels it has enough working capital, so one of my partners looks at me and asks, "You're sure you want to ship this board to Romania? Pittsburgh will give us seventeen grand for it right now."

"We made the commitment to the ministry side, and we are going to honor that." The situation reminds me of the Biblical principle of honoring God with our first fruits, and that if we do that, our vats will be overflowing.

Later that day, we procure the *same* circuit

board we had just shipped overseas, the board that Pittsburgh hoped that we had in stock. We call them with good news. I wonder what might have happened had we given in to the temptation to sell the first board to the Pittsburgh hospital. Would we have acquired the second circuit board for the Romanian hospital? I'll never know, but even if we had, we would have lost the blessing of watching God provide.

At PartsSource, all employees are owners, and salary for sales positions is a commission. The commission varies, but the principle is the same: the more they sell, the more they make, and the more the company makes. What I thought was obvious is that there is no downside to an employee who earns an enormous commission. I would love to pay a salesman a million dollars for commission: if I'm paying a million, imagine how much the company makes! Yet I've seen employers get upset when one of their salesmen has a banner month, and the boss acts as if the employee is running away with all the profits. This happened to me when I was in California during the early eighties...

I would be taking a calculated risk by leaving a safe job with decent pay to take this job in sales with half the base pay. The carrot dangling before me is, of course, the commission. I silently calculate my potential income and then pose a rhetorical question. "So, you're telling me that if I sell a million dollars of equipment, I'll have a six-figure salary?"

The director nods and says, "That's right, but I don't want to get your hopes up, Ray. Nobody's ever sold that much in a year. But as I'm sure you've already calculated, you'll earn a decent living even if you sell just half of that."

I know the medical supplies industry, I know what I am capable of, and I know I can sell a million dollars of equipment. I take the job.

One year later, I become their first salesman to top the million dollar mark. Instead of praise, awards, and write-ups in the company newsletter, all I hear are complaints about how much they are paying me. I can't even comprehend their thinking—they just sold a million dollars worth of product, and they're worried about my salary? Maybe the complaints were due to envy rather than corporate policy, but the lesson isn't lost on me.

Their attitude played a major impact in how I have viewed employees over the years: if I'm paying a commission to people who are taking risks with me, I *want* them to earn enormous sums of money.

"You can never pay an employee too many compliments."

"Compliment in public, criticize in private."

The need for motivation is also why I believe so strongly in positive reinforcement, and the impetus for my saying, *you can never pay an employee too many compliments.* Along with that is a supporting thought that needs no explanation, *compliment in public; criticize in private.*

PartsSource never was—and never will be—about me. I founded the company as a vehicle

87

for providing a valuable service to the medical community. By doing this, we serve the community by lowering the cost of health care. We save health care providers money on replacement parts so they don't have to charge as much. One can only guess how many lives might have been saved because we delivered a critical repair part overnight. PartsSource provides the community with a source of employment and fortifies the area's tax base. The money we spend collectively as a company, and individually as employees, fuels the local economy. The company's global influence is growing, too, by providing affordable (and often, free) supplies to needy providers throughout the world. It is my conviction that those are the things that the Lord requires of us, and that those who are committed to such things will be successful.

Chapter 9
The value of employees

"Just the act of listening means more than you can imagine to most employees."—Bob Nelson

I've often said that my company's best assets drive home at the end of the day. I believe that with all my heart, and that is why I go to such great extents to find the best people I can. After an extensive interview process, I meet with every potential new-hire. At PartsSource, we make our objectives clear—what we expect from an employee, and what we offer in return for their performance. We don't want square pegs trying to fill round holes. That's important, considering that for most employees, two-thirds of their waking lives are spent at work. I tell prospective employees that they have more to lose than the company does: if things don't work out for them, those moments of life vanish, never to be renewed. The company loses only money, which can be recouped. It's a prime reason I often tell people, "Our days are numbered—make sure you are happy at work."

There have been times when a new employee came aboard excited about the challenges, only to discover the job wasn't what he expected. If this employee is still sold on the company, we do everything possible to match his skills with another position. Sometimes we've gone through several positions before we find the right fit, and on rare occasions, the fit just isn't there. But usually we find the right match, and those employees are rewarded for their efforts. We also make celebration a priority, a successful business tactic too often overlooked. At PartsSource, we set manageable sales goals that allow us to celebrate regularly. Celebrations can be as simple as picnics at my home to outings at amusement parks or sporting events, all on the company's tab. Celebration reaffirms beliefs, builds camaraderie, fosters an expectant attitude of success, and it's just plain fun.

Most experts claim there are only two management styles: the carrot and the stick. The stick rules by fear, but I believe people are far more productive when enticed by a carrot, and they tend to be happier too. That's why every PartsSource employee has some type of financial bonus to work toward. After more than twenty-five years in leadership positions, from startup companies to the mega corporations, I have yet to find one instance of people flourishing in a negative environment. Yet that's the method of choice for most companies— they place their people in a "no" box and tell them what they can't do. At PartsSource, we prefer the "yes" box, where we give the employees the resources they need and let them live up to their potential. Obviously, the carrot style of management works only for motivated individuals. I can't feel sorry for those who don't want to work; besides, there are plenty of companies willing to pay a sloth what he is worth. As one who likes to make the most of

---

"Work hard at work so you can get home on time."

"Reenergize yourself before you get home; your family doesn't deserve to see the worst of you."

---

my opportunities, I offer two thoughts, *work hard at work so you can get home on time;* likewise, be at your best when you arrive home: *reenergize yourself before you get home; your family doesn't deserve to see the worst of you.*

One of the joys I've experienced is watching my oldest son Jeff excel in the medical business. I knew Jeff was a natural at sales, which is why I hired him, but I've always made it clear to him that he would receive no special treatment. That's important to me, and it goes far beyond my desire to avoid charges of nepotism. Quite simply, I don't want my children to take anything for granted, and I want them to experience trials.

One of the biggest misconceptions parents have is that struggles are inherently bad, and most don't want their kids to endure what they did. I find that amazing since it was the ability to overcome obstacles that made the parents successful. So many times I hear parents say, "I don't want my kids to struggle like I had to. I want a better life for them." Ironically, the Bible implores Christians to consider it joy when they encounter trials. Children who have the world handed to them aren't likely to develop the qualities necessary for success. Traits such as patience, discipline, persistence, self-confidence, and the ability to dream are learned. We appreciate most what we work hardest to obtain.

So when another company tried to lure Jeff away with a job that sounded too good to be true, I could only offer advice.

"Dad, they're offering me crazy money, my own Corvette and Harley, and a golf course condo."

I don't have a good feeling about this. Jeff is a great salesman, but he's too young to get an offer like that, and I certainly can't match it. "Did he give you the offer in writing?"

"Well, no… but I trust him. Even if I didn't get everything, how bad could it be?"

"Jeff, people will say almost anything to make a buck. I would be very skeptical unless you have something in writing."

"Dad, I just need to do this. I'll have more responsibility than I've ever had, I'll be in a new environment, and no one can say I only got the position because of you."

There's no way Jeff's getting those kinds of perks, but I can't stand in his way. I admire his sense of adventure, and regardless of what happens, I know he'll come away wiser for the experience. Wistful, I watch him depart.

Not long after, I get a call from Jeff, and we talk about his new job. He tries to sound upbeat, but I can tell something is up. I prod him for details, but he remains vague. Finally I ask, "So have you driven the 'Vette or the Harley yet?"

"Um, no… I don't actually have them, but I can get access to them."

I was afraid of that. "What about your condo—are you right on the golf course?"

"No, that's already filled. I've got to wait on that, so I'm staying in an apartment not far from work."

"But the owner's paying for that until you can move into the company condo?"

"Not exactly, I still have to pay, but the condo should be available soon, and then—"

I cut him off and change the subject. I don't even bother about asking him about the alleged outrageous salary; what Jeff needs now is my support. He sounds cheerful when he hangs up, but I have to believe he's bitterly disappointed. I offer a quick prayer and ask the Lord to sustain him.

Our company's carrot management style has worked amazingly well in finding our core group of employees, and it is amazing how we happen upon them. I recall a weekend during the early days of PartsSource when Jan and I attended a progressive dinner—a social event popular with churches—where couples partake of one course at each participant's home.

Eventually, our conversations turn to discussions about our vocations. When I explain to a couple next to us what our company does, I notice a guy across the room straining to hear our conversation. I describe how much I believe in the mission of PartsSource, and I mention that we need someone to direct our sales and marketing efforts. By now, it's a wonder his neck doesn't snap. I'm tempted to invite him over, but we get the call to move on to the next house. Not to my surprise, he approaches me. It's Don Hubbard, a guy I used to coach with on our sons' football team. Don shakes my hand.

"Ray, I didn't realize what your company did until today. I love the concept, and I want that job."

I wish all my hires were this easy. But I also know that Don is out of our league—he has a lot of years in sales, and there's no way we can afford him. "Don, I would love to hire you, but I can't afford it. We're just hitting our stride, and quite frankly, we just can't pay someone of your caliber."

"I don't care, I want that job. I'm serious—I can do it. That job is nearly identical to what I'm doing right now in the automotive industry."

Now he's got me thinking. If he wants the job that badly, then we ought to be able to come up with a solution. If PartsSource continues to grow at the current pace, then we could pay him top dollar at this time next year. I've been successful by surrounding myself with good people—I couldn't let a person of his experience and integrity get away. Our host interrupts, announcing that we'll have to continue our conversations at the next course.

In the driveway, Don and I talk shop. Finally, I propose my solution. "Come to work for me for now. We'll do a six-month trial—all or nothing. If you excel—and you will—I'll make you a partner; if you fall on your face—and you won't—you're gone."

Don is beaming like a real estate agent who just sold a Beverly Hills estate. "I'll take that offer," he says, "... partner."

Under Don's leadership, PartsSource tripled its sales every year. I believe that our meeting at the progressive dinner was orchestrated for a reason, and because of it, lives were changed, and a sagging local economy received a much-needed boost. God honors those who listen to His still, small voice.

Six months after Jeff left for his dream job in Georgia, he returns home in need of a job. The problem is, his position at PartsSource has been filled, and I am not about to simply hand him a job. Don Hubbard, our newly appointed Vice President of Sales and Marketing, approaches me in the hallway and says, "Ray, we're interviewing for sales people. Jeff knows this business better than anyone. If he's here to stay, let's hire him."

I raise my hands in a "keep me out of this one" gesture. "Don, I don't want to be involved with this—the last thing I need is to hear murmuring of nepotism. You're welcome to interview him, but I want you to hire the best person. You won't be doing anyone a favor if you hire him and he's not the best candidate. If he is the best available, then he reports to you. And if he doesn't meet the goals we've set, you'll have to let him go."

Don agrees and proceeds with the interviews.

As it turns out, Jeff is the best candidate so Don hires him. Jeff immerses himself into his new position with all the passion I can ask for. It's a perfect fit, and I'm relieved that everything worked out better than I could have planned. Jeff prospers under Don's mentoring, and today, Jeff is the National Sales Manager, overseeing a growing, fifty-million dollar business.

By now you know that I am a firm believer that the Lord provides for our needs, almost always in unexpected ways—often in spectacular fashion— just so we're reminded of who's really in charge. As PartsSource continued to grow, we found ourselves in need of a technical operations manager, which we knew would be a difficult position to fill. Since I've had such positive experiences with the Armed Forces and the types of people they develop, we chose to work with a recruiter who specialized in military personnel. One day I get a call from the recruiter.

"Ray, I think I found someone for you. This

guy's not only ex-military, he's a pastor! I mean, I know you've got that religious thing going..."

I smile to myself and thank him for the call. "Sounds great—what branch of the military is he with?" I ask more out of politeness than out of necessity.

"Army. But he's done a lot with medical equipment service—he's right up your alley."

"All right, then. We'll check him out."

We arrange an interview.

I immediately know he is our guy. The problem is that we can't afford him. He tells me he wants the job but feels he can't afford to work for what we are offering.

After some time passes, I call to follow up, and his wife answers the phone. I explain to her the mission of PartsSource, how it came to be, and where we hope to be in the near future. It doesn't take long to sell her on the concept, and later that day, we sign our new Technical Manager. Since then, his technical excellence and strong spiritual presence have served us beyond measure. He leads our weekly employee Bible study and is an inspirational mentor to us all.

Chapter 10
On becoming an entrepreneur

"Nothing in the world can take the place of persistence. Talent will not; nothing is more common than unsuccessful men with talent. Genius will not; unrewarded genius is almost a proverb. Education alone will not; the world is full of educated derelicts. Persistence and determination alone are omnipotent."—Calvin Coolidge

Nearly everyone loves the idea of being their own boss, especially if they can work from home, make lots of money, and have the freedom to come and go as they please. They just don't want the actual work it takes to make it happen, nor do they want the risk. If you love the lifestyle more than the occupation, you probably won't succeed. Ted Williams didn't become a great hitter by reading about it and dreaming of hitting a walk-off homer to win the game, he practiced. He took a natural talent and worked hard to hone the skill until he was the best he could be. Business is no different than any other discipline: it takes hard work and commitment, usually over a prolonged period of time.

If you're going to start a business, make sure it's something you enjoy and something that

---

"Never start a business that offers low price as its only value; there is always someone who can lose more money, longer."

"I can't make you be successful; I can only make you wish you were."

---

offers value. The lure of freedom and being your own boss sometimes tempts people into making bad decisions. If you don't have a passion for your work, how do you expect customers or employees to love what you do? And, if your product or service isn't better than everything else available, who will want it? If you want to run a business, consider this: *never start a business that offers low price as its only value; there is always someone who can lose more money, longer;* and, *I can't make you successful; I can only make you wish you were.*

Even the most opportunistic entrepreneur is likely to need years to be successful. Unfortunately, most people want it all—now—and they don't want to be bothered with a lot of extra work. Get rich quick schemes are nothing new of course, and they will always be with us. It amazes me at the number of work from home programs that claim to pay up to twenty thousand dollars a month. Who would have thought that stuffing envelopes could be so lucrative? I've always paid a fair wage to my employees, and I have always included incentives, but I've never paid anyone two hundred grand for licking envelopes or surfing the Web.

What I've noticed about entrepreneurs is that most are idea-driven and are not afraid to dream; they are typically opportunistic and are not afraid to act quickly when necessary, they are confident of their abilities and are not afraid of hard work and long hours. Ultimately, they are not afraid to take a calculated risk because without risk, there is no reward. Notice I mention a *calculated* risk. The trick is to minimize that risk. Everyone should have a healthy fear of failure, but if the specter of failure paralyzes you, you'll never succeed. I hate risks, but I'm willing to take a risk as long as I understand the outcome if I fail. Successful entrepreneurs minimize their risk by preparation and analysis so that they stack the deck in their favor.

Some people are averse to any risk. There's nothing wrong with that, but they'll never be successful on their own until they conquer that fear. I recall a conversation I had with two men who had been quite successful in medical sales. After describing my vision for a new product I want to offer, I methodically explain each element of the operation and how I plan to make it work. Their nodding heads affirm my belief that this business has incredible potential.

"I'm so convinced this will work," I tell them,

"that I'm willing to finance the whole thing. All I need are champions, and that's where you two come in." I expect to see their eyes light up like Christmas trees, but their silence and looks of hesitation tell me I haven't been so convincing.

"And that means we have to quit our jobs," the first one says.

I shrug. "A minor tradeoff for a chance to make your fortune."

The second budding entrepreneur chimes in with, "I don't know, Ray, it sounds good, but I'm already doing well with my current job—I hate to risk it all for something that's uncertain."

I look him in the eye in an obvious challenge and then begin my line of reasoning. "Can you tell me one thing about my plan that isn't realistic?"

Both men shake their heads, and the second one mumbles a "no."

"And you agree that if we do most of the principles I've outlined, we would make money."

They nod in agreement.

"Guys, if you offered me this opportunity—you front the money while I run the show—I would be all over it!"

"Ray," the first salesman manages, "it really is a good plan, and it probably would make everyone a lot of money. But nothing in life is guaranteed."

I can't argue that. But an attitude of calculated reason separates the entrepreneurs from captive employees. If you've reasoned through five scenarios, and you've got four that support your decision, the entrepreneur makes that move. Even if one situation goes awry, you still have four in your favor. I've read that the U.S. Marines use this principle: when they make a plan, they act upon it the moment that seventy percent of the information supports that decision. Their experience is that if you sit and wait, you die.

Nothing in this world is guaranteed, including the jobs those two have now. But as the saying goes, nothing ventured, nothing gained. Will these men one day look back and rue the fact they turned down a life-changing opportunity? I can speak from experience that most people who place themselves at risk in an entrepreneurial position gain an incredible amount of motivation to succeed. When a person's financial future hinges on the results of his labor, that person won't need much motivation to make that happen. At some point, you have to have enough confidence in yourself to know you'll find a way to make it happen.

> *"The 4 E's of successful entrepreneurship: evaluation, effort, energy, effect."*

The E's of Entrepreneurship

In many of my speaking engagements, I speak of the four E's of becoming a successful entrepreneur:

Evaluation—where are people spending money?

Effort—are you willing to expend the extra effort to understand the problem?

Energy—are you willing to do what it takes?

Effect—can you measure the effects so that you know your effort works?

The first E, evaluation, should be obvious but might be the most overlooked way to establish a business. So many people ask, 'How do you come up with so many good ideas to grow businesses?' Like most entrepreneurs, I have no problem coming up with ideas to create business. I have more ideas than I have time for, and I get most of those ideas by following the money. I did that when I worked for the hospital in California: I followed the money by observing how private practice physicians acquired their supplies. When I discovered they were paying top dollar for medical supplies, I used the resources I had to offer them the same supplies at a reduced cost. I simply improved one of their necessary transactions. Any time you can increase the satisfaction of a purchase, you have the makings of a successful business.

The second E is effort. Those who want to succeed on their own must be willing to spend the time to understand their business. Most entrepreneurs go into business in their field of expertise, but it's not unusual for the business side to require vastly different skills from those in which they have been trained. A skilled finish carpenter might be capable of creating filigree suitable for a palace, yet it wouldn't be unthinkable for him to fail miserably if he goes into the home improvement business for himself. I've seen great engineers struggle when they're "promoted" to management. That shouldn't surprise anyone; the skill sets are different. There aren't a lot of people who are naturally talented in more than one discipline.

The third E is energy. It takes work to create your own business, usually a lot of work. In most cases, budding entrepreneurs must work a full-time job while they try their hand at their new enterprise during off hours. What is your dream worth to you—are you willing to sacrifice personal time, sleep less, and work more? Are you willing to learn new skills and study aspects of your industry that might ordinarily bore you? Are you willing to expand your expertise in multiple disciplines, or will you only do what is fun? Do you have a trusted core of people you can go to for advice and emotional support? No business is the same, so some require more time than others, but the old saying holds true here: if it were easy, everyone would be doing it.

The fourth E is effect. It's critical for entrepreneurs to measure their success. If they try something new, they need to know what effect that had. Most entrepreneurs wear many hats, so time and money are valuable commodities. If you want to be an entrepreneur, you can't waste resources—it's critical to know what works and what doesn't. It might cost money to do this; spend it. If you don't know what works, you'll find out the hard way what doesn't.

"Innovation is like rearranging chairs on a deck—the owner loves the new look and you get to keep a few chairs for yourself."

People often refer to me as a serial entrepreneur. I'm honored by the title, but I consider myself more of an innovator than an entrepreneur. It's a difference in attitude: the entrepreneur wants to make money, while the innovator wants to change things. That desire to change things—to make a product better or to improve a service or transaction—has led me to entrepreneurial opportunities. It also led to a life-lesson, *innovation is like rearranging chairs on someone's deck—the owner loves the new look and you get to keep a few for yourself.*

My desire to improve health care services resulted in many changes: providers saved money (which sometimes led to adding or retaining personnel), my company provided jobs and contributed tax dollars to the community, and I profited professionally, financially, and spiritually. The world longs for the secret to riches, because people believe that wealth will bring them joy. It may offer temporary happiness, but never joy and contentment. Contentment is a spiritual issue, and nobody will ever be truly fulfilled unless they have a personal relationship with Jesus Christ. If ever there has been something I've been right about, this is it—no Christian ever regretted living out his faith to its fullest.

For those who want to become an entrepreneur, I ask, "What is your motivation?" There's nothing wrong about wanting more, as long as you've learned to be content with what you have. Most people never understand that if they haven't learned to be content with what they have, they'll never be content—even if they own the entire world. King Solomon discovered that thousands of years ago when, as the richest man in the world, he went through a period of discontentment. To remedy that, Solomon gave himself everything that caught his fancy, and he held nothing back. Predictably, he was more miserable than before. Riches cannot satisfy. Mathematician Blaise Pascal once said that inside every man is a God-shaped vacuum that only He can fill. Most of us try to fill it with more of our self, but our selfish desires only serve to make that hole bigger.

If you have a burning desire to become an entrepreneur, by all means do it—you'll regret it if you don't. The life offers freedom, joy, self-satisfaction, and rewards beyond measure. But just make sure you have the proper motives. If you are merely trying to fill that God-shaped hole, there are less expensive ways to fail.

Chapter 11
Success is not by accident

"The harder you work, the harder it is to surrender."—Vince Lombardi

The world longs for the secret to happiness and riches. There are untold numbers of books on the subject, and nearly as many classes, conferences, and seminars that promise a short cut to success. I'm a believer that every human being is here for a reason. God has given each of us unique talents, and it is His desire that we use them for honorable purposes. Our abilities are merely gifts from God, so it is foolish to boast about our accomplishments. As a steward, I want to make the most of my limited time on this planet. There are plenty of people who use their gifts for selfish purposes and never recognize the true giver of those gifts. While some of those experienced success at the expense of others, most are where they are because they have worked hard and made good business decisions. Regardless of how they achieved financial success, I am convinced they will never be truly content if they do not address their spiritual needs. It is the spiritual aspect of my life that drives me and guides my success.

While my spiritual life guides me in the direction I need to go, there is no substitute for work. I've seen people who hide behind their Christianity and act as if they never need to do anything. They repeat phrases such as, "I'll just wait on the Lord to provide," when what they really mean is they don't feel like doing the work to meet the need. I would be the first to defend the need for trusting God for our provisions, but part of that trust entails doing everything in our power to make things happen. I believe the Bible is clear about our need to take action: we do the work and trust God for the results. The Bible also makes it clear that God rewards all of our labor done for Him, whether that is building a shelter for an impoverished family or acquiring an X-ray tube.

One of the reasons I have a passion for what I do is because I am convinced that it's what God wants me to do. Thanks to Bob Pagett's challenge to me when we were in Romania, I've dedicated myself to becoming "an Ephesians 2:10 guy." It's clear that God has appointed us to work in such a way that betters our world, and that He prepared us for that. When I look back on my life's circumstances, I see how events were actually pieces of a puzzle that now fit together. At the time, however, many of those pieces were just puzzling.

I'm not alone in the belief that people are amazingly confident when they are doing what they believe is their life-appointed work, and that confidence energizes them to do things they might never have thought possible. Some equate confidence with arrogance, but I believe that people exude a quiet confidence when they allow the Lord to use their talents for His work. These are reasons I believe so strongly in what I do, and why I approach my work with confidence and the joy of knowing my work—like everyone who dedicates their efforts to the Lord—makes a difference.

"The five C's of success: confidence, credibility, compliment, community, and communication."

Anyone who has attended a motivational conference where I've been the speaker has heard me mention the three C's of success—confidence, credibility, and communication. Since then, I've decided there are really five C's—including compliment and community—which are simply my abbreviated outline for success. I'm sure these same principles have been explained in other ways, but since I can remember five C's, the concept works for me. I'm successful when I follow the principle of the five C's, so naturally I try to surround myself with others who espouse the same belief.

The first C, confidence, is simply knowing that you can do it. People are confident when they've experienced triumph, but conversely, it's difficult to be confident in something you've never experienced. Equipment repair is an example of this: the thought of repairing a costly machine unnerves a lot of potential service people, but after they do it, their confidence grows exponentially. The more victories people experience, the more confident they become about their abilities, and the more likely they are to repeat their success. In time, confidence expands beyond the familiar. The person who successfully services equipment goes on to tackle more difficult tasks because his experience shows him how the process works. A simple repair leads to refurbishing more complex equipment; after all, if he messes up the repair, he knows how to rebuild the entire machine. Eventually, that technician might even start an equipment sales business based on his succession of small victories.

Some people confuse confidence with cockiness,

but there's a marked contrast between the brash personalities of those who are really just insecure, and the quiet confidence of those who are self-assured. Truly confident people aren't yearning for someone to notice them, and those are the kind of employees I want. Confidence breeds success. Most self-starters are confident of their abilities and aren't afraid to try new things. They don't need constant supervision, and they aren't afraid to fail. When confident employees do fail, they chalk it up to a learning experience and then try again. Confident employees find ways to get the job done.

The second C is credibility, which is simply a history of success. Those who are repeatedly successful gain credibility in their field. Naturally, credibility is predicated on the first C, confidence: confident people are successful, and hence, gain credibility. But credibility is more than just doing a good job; it's keeping one's word. Credible people do what they say they will do. Credible people have convictions—you know where they stand, and you'll rarely be surprised by what they do. Credible people are honest.

The third C is compliment. I'm a firm believer that you can never compliment someone too much. Nobody tires of hearing praise, and like giving, it makes the giver feel good too. Acknowledge accomplishments. Learn to celebrate victories. Even a minor victory is cause for celebration and is worthy of a few words of praise. Don't be afraid to whoop it up once in awhile—bump chests, high-five, and have fun seeing others succeed. Success is made to be shared; it's no fun to pat yourself on the back—you need others. Conversely, others need your energy to revitalize them. The most common reason employees state for leaving their place of employment is a perceived lack of respect. Nobody wants to be taken for granted. A little praise goes a long way. Not every employee will be a superstar, but each does have a unique gift. Take the effort to notice those talents, and tell people what you appreciate about them.

The fourth C is community. Give joyfully to your community—donate to worthy charities, give of yourself as a volunteer, or find some way to get involved. Good things happen when people commit to their community: their efforts influence people directly and indirectly. Leaders have the potential to change the lives of those they work with, and one can only guess at their sphere of influence when you consider the multiplication effect.

Dr. Billy Graham has given his message of hope to millions of people—many of whom have since experienced radically changed lives. And those whose lives were changed often passed along their experience to others, and so on until it became impossible to count all that was done. And so I wonder how many people influenced Dr. Graham? Maybe it was a Sunday school teacher who was merely being faithful, week after week, who spurred a young Billy Graham to do great things. Since I never know who I might influence, I am compelled to do my best in whatever I do. Who did Abraham Lincoln model himself after that made him such a man of character? Oh, that I might influence someone of purpose and commitment. I'll be watchful, though; I don't want to be the one they look back on, like a child spurned by his parents, and say, "I hope I'm never like him."

The fifth C is communication. Tell everyone you know about what you do and the people you surround yourself with—the more passion you convey, the greater your impact. Excitement is contagious. People love to be around those who have a positive outlook, but I've never known anyone who enjoys hanging around with whiners. Who wants to listen to complaints and excuses?

If you're an employer, surround yourself with trusted people who will tell you the truth, good or bad. I'm amazed at the number of high-ranking company officials—I won't call them leaders—who refuse to seek counsel because they either think they know it all, or they are afraid that underlings might

> *"Always deliver the good news with a smile; always deliver the bad news with a plan."*

think less of them for not having all the answers. Nobody wants a "yes man," and no employee wants to hear fluff that's been filtered through rose colored glasses. I have a Rayism for that: *always deliver the good news with a smile; always deliver the bad news with a plan.* That not only sets the tone for a leader, it offers hope. It's a lot easier to deal with a problem if there is hope for a solution.

The few people who honestly believe that success is just a matter of luck, or a result of which family we were born into, will probably never understand the need for hard work. Most people I've met, however, understand it completely. Their unwillingness to sacrifice is the reason they *choose* not to be successful: the path is too difficult. Every person has a unique definition of success, and for most, it won't be the life of an entrepreneur. The entrepreneurial lifestyle is not for everyone, but it is the life I've chosen and is one that my family supports. Entrepreneurship provides me with tremendous personal satisfaction because it allows me to use my God-given abilities to make a difference in this world.

Chapter 12
Reaping what you sow

"Sow a thought, and you reap an act; sow an act, and you reap a habit; sow a habit, and you reap a character; sow a character, and you reap a destiny." —Charles Reader

I never claim to have arrived at perfection. I'm a flawed, fallible human no different than everyone else on the planet. But after years of suffering, scrimping, saving, and eking out an existence, my labors have paid off, and now I'm enjoying the bounty of the abundant life that Christ promises.

Over the years, I have been the recipient of many awards and accolades; however, in 2004

Ernst & Young awarded me their Entrepreneur of the Year award—what I consider my crowning professional achievement. And this from a kid who worked at a gas station when I thought that was as much as I could expect out of life! Thirty years ago I couldn't have fathomed my life today. I am incredibly fortunate to have the material and spiritual blessings I do, and I do my best not to flaunt them. After all, I'm merely the steward using resources I've been called to manage.

I run a tight ship with my business, and we are careful to spend wisely. If we can save significant money on used shelving, why not? It's as good as new, and nobody sees it in a warehouse. It's fun to relate my business philosophy to my less-than-

> *"I run my business like the way I play golf; I keep my cost per stroke as low as possible."*

stellar golf game. I tell people that I'm a value golfer—if I'm going to pay for the privilege of chasing a ball around, then I'm going to get my money's worth. My tongue-in-cheek response to conversations about the sport is, *I run my business the way I play golf; I keep my cost per stroke as low as possible.*

But after all these years and circumstances—light years removed from my former life in Watts, some things never change. The most important consistency is I still date my wife each week. It's a special time for us to share our hearts, laugh, and just appreciate the gift that God has given us in each

> *"If you don't date your spouse, someone else will."*

other. I frequently remind men, especially busy executives, of this important Rayism, *date your wife, or somebody else will.* A regularly scheduled time together tells her that she's important. My wife is my first responsibility, and she takes precedence over my job and even over the kids. If my relationship with Jan is out of sync, then the rest of my life will be out of order. Marriage is like an emotional nest egg, and I guard it like the treasure it is.

Another thing that hasn't changed is my frugalness. While we don't have to clip coupons anymore, we are always stewards of our resources, sometimes to a fault. It's not as if we have to pinch pennies, but I believe God has blessed us beyond measure because we want to live in a reasonable manner. We even bought our house based on its potential. It needed work, but its near-wilderness setting was perfect for our needs. I solicited bids for the extensive work we needed, and I did much of it myself. Now our home blends with the natural surroundings and creates a quiet refuge refreshing to the soul. The chatter of a chickadee, the scent of a white pine, and the spectacle of the fox dallying in our brook are worth far more than the McMansion fortresses that some love to showcase.

We use our home for church and company gatherings, but we never serve alcohol. I'm not opposed to drinking in moderation, but the consumption of alcohol does send a message, and it's not one I ordinarily want to portray, certainly not in a business setting. PartsSource doesn't reimburse for alcohol. Our sales people aren't forbidden to have a drink with a client, but the expense is their own. My philosophy has always been to include celebration—it's good to celebrate our small victories so we can build on them and instill an attitude of success. Alcohol is prevalent in our society, but that doesn't mean it's necessarily the best choice for a party. I've noticed that when people gather, they have fun regardless of the refreshments—it's the fellowship they long for. Everyone enjoys time spent with friends.

Each of us is unique in our background, experiences, and talents, so it only stands to reason that each will have different levels of success. So many of the factors that determine success are beyond our control, but we can control our integrity. Our integrity is who we really are, because it's what's hidden in our heart. Are we, as Jesus described the deceitful religious leaders of his day, merely whitewashed tombs—clean on the outside but full of decay inside? Or as J. C. Watts has asked, what is it that we do when no one is looking? Nobody is perfect, and everyone fails daily in one form or another, but a desire to maintain our integrity should be a character trait every successful person longs for.

I am confident that my success is founded on telling the truth—even when it's not convenient, keeping my word, and resolving to always do what is right. If I am committed to truth, I'll sleep well because I will never worry about mixing up my stories. The high road is never easy, but it's always right. People prosper when they are above reproach, and success always follows. Many people may say otherwise, but I believe that deep down, everyone desires to have impeccable character. But as the saying goes, if it were easy, everyone would be doing it. Like discipline, a blameless character comes at a cost, but its blessings are beyond measure. I've never met anyone who wished he hadn't worked so hard to be honest and trustworthy.

Chapter 13
Dare to dream

"Twenty years from now you will be more disappointed by the things that you didn't do than by the ones you did do. So throw off the bowlines. Sail away from the safe harbor. Catch the trade winds in your sails. Explore. Dream. Discover."—Mark Twain

There is a popular line of thinking—typically by those who dream of winning a lottery—that once we obtain the American Dream and have enough money for life, we sit back and enjoy it. I'm not sure I would know how to do that. Besides, that line of thinking is simply not true, at least from a Biblical standpoint. Even if it were true, that lifestyle would hardly be fulfilling. As stated by my life verse, Ephesians 2:10, we are created for a purpose, and I plan to serve my Lord as long as I draw breath. That's what drives me. So what's the difference between my motivation and that of most people?

Many people are driven by some form of self-gratification, and it's often so subtle that people never realize it. It's a powerful motivator, but the problem is pleasing only ourselves can never fulfill our deepest needs. That's why there are so many successful business people who appear to have the world by the tail, but they lost their souls long ago. Though their bank accounts flourish, their marriages and relationships fail; they lead lives, as Thoreau once said, of quiet desperation. God wants us to prosper in every way, and all He asks of us is our faith and obedience. That flies in the face of the unbeliever, because to those who make no room for the power of God, it's simply not possible to give up control of our life and expect to reap rewards. Yet it happens every day, and it's happened to me since I made that decision so many years ago. It defies logic only if your view of logic precludes the supernatural. Our God is bigger than man's limited view of what is possible.

So that's why I never want to stop learning, and giving, and loving, and doing all the things a servant of Christ is called to do. Like every Christian who has ever lived, I've failed my God, and yet He has never failed me. That's why I persevere—I'm merely being faithful with the talents God has given me. It's easier to serve a cause bigger than yourself, and it's far more rewarding than yielding to selfish desires. Isn't it odd how we are instinctively repulsed by braggarts and self-centered people, yet our natural tendency is to focus solely on ourselves? We notice self-centeredness in everyone but ourselves.

When I speak at conferences, my desire is for people to see the passion I have for life, and for my life's work. Do you love what you do for a living? You should. Our lives are too short to be miserable at something that consumes most of our waking hours. Many people merely settle for a job; they don't necessarily hate it, but they don't have a passion for it either. I believe it's possible to have a job you love, but it might mean taking some risks to find it. I've seen plenty of people who hang on to a miserable situation because it's familiar. Most would never admit it, but the truth is they are simply afraid to find something else because they are afraid to fail. I would rather fail at attempting great things than succeed in attaining mediocrity.

For Christians, there really is no excuse for not seeking a fulfilling career, because the Bible implores us to live lives free of fear and worry. Two of my favorite verses to claim are: *2 Timothy 1:7— For God did not give us a spirit of timidity, but a spirit of power, of love and self-discipline;* and *Philippians 4:6-7—Do not be anxious about anything, but in everything by prayer and petition, with thanksgiving, present your requests to God. And the peace of God, which transcends all understanding, will guard your hearts and your minds in Christ Jesus.*

Too many people don't have this hope, but I would implore them with the simplest of arguments, what do you have to lose? If it's the devil you do know versus the devil you don't know syndrome, at least the unknown devil offers an adventure, even if only temporarily.

As to public speaking, I'll continue to do that as long as organizations invite me. For me, public speaking is as natural as breathing because it allows me to talk from the heart, and few things are more satisfying. Plus, it is such a joy when I can inspire others. When you learn news that's too good to keep to yourself, you can't help telling everyone you see. I'm convinced that's it's never too late to seek your life's adventure, so count on the fact I'll spend the rest of my life encouraging others to do just that.

As you set about your adventure, don't forget that most of the excitement is in the journey—learn to enjoy your daily segment of the trip. It's almost amusing how so many people act as if they are the only one who has ever had problems. Everyone has problems; we're just too busy focused on our own troubles to notice the pain of our neighbors. So expect difficulties, and then make the most of the ride. After all, you don't want to get to the end too soon!

Chapter 14
Where do I go from here?

"Here is a test to see if your mission on earth is finished. If you are alive, it isn't."—Francis Bacon

I've lived a life that most people would consider adventurous and successful, and every day I remind myself not to take it for granted. I know what it's like to live in abject poverty and hopelessness, and I know what it's like to rub shoulders with the rich and famous. I've had more blessings than I deserve, but I continually remain thankful to the God that has molded me into a vessel He can use.

Where will life take me next? For now, my life mission is to continue being the best innovator and motivator I can be. I have plans for new business ventures, which may or may not include me. Will I ever be able to stop creating companies? That remains to be seen. I do have an interest in politics, and my life experiences certainly make me qualified for political office. During my life, I've experienced facets of life that concern people most about our country: education, the economy, family, social programs, and the military.

So why would I want to take a pay cut to endure constant scrutiny, criticism, and the bureaucratic morass of our Federal government? I love my country. I am proud of my service in the Air Force that shaped me during my formative years, I have a passion for where I believe we need to be as a nation, and I believe I can make a difference. On the other hand, I've heard influential business people say that I have so many convictions I couldn't even get elected, much less be successful in politics.

As a man of principle, I take that as a compliment, which is exactly how they meant it. But I've heard that argument for years, and I believe a person of conviction can hold a political office—you just have to pick your battles. There are some issues in which you simply cannot compromise because they are the core of your belief and who you are; other items of debate are merely disagreements over what is important. I always hold fast to my principles, but I am willing to compromise on matters that aren't critical.

How is that attitude different from every other politician? For those without any conviction, it's radically different. There are too many so-called public servants who are more concerned about themselves than about their constituents. I don't doubt that many came to elected office with good intentions, but the daily pressures of party bosses and the trappings of power have ways of turning one's heart. Nobody is immune, but a person of conviction is least likely to cave. A major problem in government is there are too many representatives who have no core beliefs; they determine their position by the prevailing winds of public opinion.

While I've never held the office of an elected official, I do have experience with the temptations they face. By God's grace, I've endured the lure of questionable financial gain; I know what it's like to be in positions of power and what that can do to a man. The moment of temptation is the wrong time to form a conviction. That's why I guard my heart against temptation by studying Scripture and by avoiding situations that might compromise my faith. As an example, I never ride in a car where I am alone with a woman other than my wife. Even though I know there would never be a problem, I make sure I avoid even the appearance · of impropriety. People are less likely to gossip if there's nothing to gossip about, but there are a lot of politicians who have come to ruin by ignoring this basic principle.

Whenever anyone mentions politics, the polarizing issue of political party comes into play. There are many registered political parties in the U.S., but the reality is that the Big Two have a stranglehold on the elective process. The political experts analyze party differences to the nth degree, but I remember a simpler commentary of how Democrats and Republicans agree on one thing: both want your money; they just disagree on how to spend it. As much as I prefer a more even playing field than our current system offers, I wouldn't try to change the two-party system. The arrangement is too entrenched, and there are not enough days in a lifetime to change that. If I ever hold an elected office, I would simply try to be an honorable member.

The biggest adjustment for me would be overcoming the glacial speed at which the government works. As one who is used to making things happen quickly in private industry, I would have to adjust to political machination that is about as nimble as a cow on roller skates. The only good thing about that is it saves the nation from all the harm it might do if it could act quickly. So as much as I would love to speed up the process, maybe I should be careful what I wish for.

So what would my platform be? If you've heard me speak or read this book through up to this point, you probably know how I would vote on most issues. I'm a natural innovator, so of course I have a lot of ideas, but comprehensive explanations are beyond the scope of this book. If indeed I do make a serious run for office, I might write another book to detail my beliefs and plans for our nation.

Whatever I do, I'll do to the best of my ability. I'll always have a special place in my heart for the health care of the nation, but regardless of my occupation, I simply want to know I've done everything possible to leave this world a better place than when I found it. I want my legacy to be a simple one: that people can say, "Ray loved the Lord." And on that day when my life's work on earth is complete, I hope to hear the words every believer longs to hear, "Well done, thou good and faithful servant."

Until then, I'll proceed with confidence.

Chapter 15
Rayisms

"*The integrity of a man is fully tested when money is involved.*"—Ray Dalton

My story wouldn't be complete without some of my most frequently repeated phrases. If you ever hear me speak, count on hearing at least some of these. They may never go down in history as the most profound words ever uttered, but they are nuggets of truth wrapped in experience and insight. They are fun for me—they roll off the tongue and are easy to remember for my speaking engagements. Since I've expounded on most of these sayings, I'll leave you with just the Rayisms, in no particular order—take them for what they are worth:

1. Rational thinking prevails.

2. Where there's chaos, there's profit.

3. Innovation is like rearranging chairs on a deck—the owner loves the new look and you get to keep a few chairs for yourself.

4. I run my business like the way I play golf; I keep my cost per stroke as low as possible.

5. Manage your work with the intensity that you manage your life.

6. Our days are numbered—make sure you are happy at work.

7. Find something about your boss that you respect, and he will learn to respect you.

8. Always deliver the good news with a smile; always deliver the bad news with a plan

9. Never bring someone a problem without offering your idea of how to solve it.

10. The person closest to the problem may have the best solution.

11. The integrity of a man is fully tested when money is involved.

12. The selling starts when the customer says no.

13. People become repeat customers when you solve their problems.

14. No order is complete until you say, "Thank You."

15. Add stock options to every employee compensation plan and you'll have a company run by owners rather than renters.

16. A man is known by the integrity of his word.

17. Treat everyone with kindness; you never know when you might have to work for them.

18. You can never pay an employee too many compliments.

19. Compliment in public, criticize in private.

20. The 4 E's of successful entrepreneurship: evaluation, effort, energy, effect.

21. The five C's of success: confidence, credibility, compliment, community, and communication.

22. Good ideas usually follow the money.

23. Growth businesses are those that solve problems.

24. Never start a business that offers low price as its only value; there is always someone who can lose more money, longer.

25. If you don't date your spouse, someone else will.

26. Work hard at work so you can get home on time.

27. Reenergize yourself before you get home; your family doesn't deserve to see the worst of you.

28. I can't make you be successful; I can only make you wish you were.

29. Excellent customer service always results in profit.

30. The customer *isn't* always right, but he's still the customer.